Disclaimer

The information provided in this book is intended for educational and informational purposes only. It is not intended to be a substitute for professional medical advice, diagnosis, or treatment. Always seek the advice of your physician or other qualified health provider with any questions you may have regarding a medical condition. Never disregard professional medical advice or delay in seeking it because of something you have read in this book.

The author and publisher of this book make no representations or warranties concerning the accuracy, applicability, fitness, or completeness of the contents of this book. They disclaim any warranties (expressed or implied), merchantability, or fitness for any particular purpose. The author and publisher shall in no event be held liable for any loss or other damages, including but not limited to special, incidental, consequential, or other damages.

Readers are encouraged to consult their healthcare provider before embarking on any holistic approach and practices discussed in this book, particularly if they are undergoing treatment for cancer or have any pre-existing medical conditions.

MINDING YOUR MIND

THE **ULTIMATE GUIDE** TO EMPOWERING A RESILIENT **MIND** ON THE JOURNEY THROUGH CANCER

SAGAR SURESH PATIL

notionpress.com

INDIA · SINGAPORE · MALAYSIA

ISBN 979-8-89363-297-2

Contents

Preface

In crafting this comprehensive guide on navigating the challenging journey of cancer, I have embarked on a mission to provide a beacon of understanding, resilience, and empowerment. As we delve into the pages that follow, the purpose becomes clear to not only inform but to uplift and guide you through journey of cancer.

I have seen firsthand the significant influence that a positive outlook and mindfulness practice can have on health outcomes beyond prescription drugs and treatments, Drawing from my two decades of experience in the medicinal field, many years of experience as a pharmacist, and my role as a loving caregiver deeply involved in every step of my family member's cancer journey. I firmly believe that overall healing and well-being can be greatly enhanced by practicing mindfulness and maintaining a happy mindset using integrated holistic approach. Stressing these techniques has not only aided in my loved one's recuperation but has also encouraged resiliency in the face of difficulties.

I also exhort everyone to recognize the benefits of adopting an optimistic outlook and utilizing it in conjunction with medical interventions. Holistic approach, Practices of mindfulness and awareness of the present moment can be quite helpful on the journey for both caregiver as well as patient. This book is not merely a collection of words but a heartfelt guide, a symphony of wisdom, and a testament to the strength within each person and their support group facing the challenges of cancer.

This book emphasize on a harmonious integration of various elements to promote healing and overall health in the journey of cancer. May this journey bring illumination, empowerment, and solace to those in search of understanding and resilience.

Sagar patil

Unlocking the Harmony of Healing

--—⦾⦿⦾—--

Understanding and exploring Cancer and mind.

"In the symphony of life, Cancer song beats tune cells awry and a smooth flow, treatment song hopes rhythm sweet and melody in tow."

"I guess cancer has been pronounced or spelled wrong...it has to be cansur....it means you can survive..."

Every diagnosed patient should go through the word "simultaneous remission" on the internet, a rare phenomenon that sometimes shows the remission or improvement of cancer on its own without any involvement of specific treatment.

This shows that the body has an innate ability to repair itself by activating and strengthening its immune system.

"Yes, the body can treat and heal itself. It's possible!"

Understanding cancer is similar to unravelling the secrets of a formidable opponent. Coping with cancer is not just about the body. But it encompasses the mind and spirit. Embracing cancer from a holistic perspective means recognizing the interconnectedness of mental, emotional, and physical health in the face of illness and adversity.

From a holistic perspective, cancer is often viewed as a complex manifestation of imbalances in the body encompassing physical, mental, and emotional aspects. It's seen not just as isolated cellular abnormalities but also as a result of a compromised overall well-being including lifestyle, stress, and environmental factors, which makes a cell order less. Unhealthy dietary habits, including excessive consumption of processed foods, red meats, and sugary beverages, coupled with an inadequate intake of fruits, vegetables, and fibre, all these above factors have been associated with heightened cancer risk. Additionally, leading a sedentary lifestyle, being overweight or obese, and indulging in excessive alcohol consumption are also recognized as risk factors for cancer development.

Believing that cancer can happen to anyone, regardless of precautions taken, can indeed be a humbling realization. While certain lifestyle choices and preventive measures can reduce the risk of developing cancer, there are still factors beyond our control, such as genetic predispositions and environmental influences that can contribute to its development.

In this context, having faith can play a role in coping with the uncertainty and challenges that cancer presents. Faith can take various forms, including spiritual beliefs, trust in the medical team, its support group, family, and confidence in one's ability to navigate the cancer journey. For some, faith provides a source of comfort, hope, and resilience in the face of illness and adversity.

However, it's essential to recognize that faith alone does not determine one's risk of developing cancer or influence the outcome of treatment. Cancer is a complex disease influenced by a combination of genetic, environmental, and lifestyle factors, and medical interventions play a crucial role in diagnosis, treatment, and management.

While faith can provide emotional and spiritual support, it's essential for individuals affected by cancer to also access appropriate medical care, support services, and resources to address their physical, emotional, and psychological needs. By integrating faith with evidence-based medical care, individuals can approach the cancer journey with a perspective that promotes healing and enhances well-being.

Exposure to environmental toxins, such as air and water pollutants, industrial chemicals, pesticides, and heavy metals can contribute to the onset of cancer. These harmful substances are pervasive in our surroundings, including the air we breathe, the water we drink, and the food we consume. Accumulation of these pollutants in the body over time can lead to cellular damage and mutations, fostering the growth of cancerous cells.

Smoking tobacco is widely acknowledged as a major cause of various cancers, such as lung, throat, and mouth cancers. Additionally, exposure to second-hand smoke or passive smoke has been linked to an increased risk of cancer development.

Overexposure to ultraviolet radiation from sunlight or artificial sources like tanning beds can inflict DNA damage on skin cells elevating the risk of skin cancer, including melanoma, which is the most lethal form of skin cancer.

Certain chemicals present in everyday products, such as plastics, cosmetics, and household cleaners have the potential to disrupt the body's hormonal balance. Prolonged exposure to these endocrine disruptors may increase the likelihood of hormone-related cancers, including breast and prostate cancer.

Some professions entail exposure to carcinogenic substances, such as asbestos, benzene, and formaldehyde, which can heighten the risk of developing specific types of cancer. Occupational exposure to these hazardous substances underscores the importance of workplace safety measures to mitigate cancer risks.

Cancer patients may experience a range of secondary problems or complications, which can vary depending on factors such as the type and stage of cancer, treatment modalities, and individual health status.

Chemotherapy, radiation therapy, surgery, various oral medications, and other cancer treatments can cause a variety of side effects, including fatigue, nausea, vomiting, hair loss, pain, neuropathy, and changes in appetite or weight. Certain types of cancer and its treatment can lead to physical symptoms such as sleep disturbances, difficulty breathing, digestive issues, urinary problems, sexual dysfunction, and skin issues.

Some cancer patients may experience cognitive changes, often referred to as "chemo brain" or "cancer-related cognitive impairment," which can include problems with memory, concentration, attention, and decision-making.

Cancer and its treatment can affect a person's ability to eat, digest, and absorb nutrients, leading to malnutrition, weight loss, or nutritional deficiencies. This can weaken the immune system, increasing the risk of infections and delaying healing from injuries or surgeries.

Many cancer patients experience emotional and psychological challenges such as anxiety, depression, fear, grief, and stress related to their diagnosis, treatment, and uncertainty about the future.

Cancer treatment and related expenses, such as medical bills, medications, transportation, and lost income, can create financial strain for patients and their families, leading to additional stress and worry.

Cancer can impact social relationships, employment, and daily activities, leading to feelings of isolation, loneliness, and changes in family dynamics and social support networks. They may grapple with existential questions, spiritual beliefs, and existential distress related to mortality, meaning-making, and the search for purpose and hope in the face of illness.

Addressing these secondary problems often requires a multidisciplinary approach involving healthcare providers, psychologists, social workers, nutritionists, physical therapists, and other supportive care professionals. By addressing both the physical and psychosocial needs of cancer patients, healthcare teams can help improve quality of life and overall well-being throughout the cancer journey.

Holistic approaches may emphasize a comprehensive healing strategy incorporating conventional medical treatments alongside efforts to support the body's natural healing mechanisms through nutrition, stress management, and emotional well-being

In conventional cancer treatment, the primary responsibility lies with the medical professionals and healthcare institutions with minimal involvement from the patient and their family. In contrast, a holistic approach emphasizes the active participation of both the patient and their caregivers in the treatment process and journey throughout the cancer. This dual approach recognizes the potential synergies that can arise from combining medical interventions with patient and family engagement, fostering a more comprehensive and integrated response to the challenges of cancer care. Such an approach may contribute to a more positive treatment outcome by addressing not only the physical aspects of the disease but also the psychosocial and lifestyle factors that can impact overall well-being.

While conventional medical treatments focus on the body's battle with cancer, a holistic approach acknowledges that it's not merely a physical challenge but also an emotional and mental one. Integrating medical treatments with healthy lifestyle choices such as sleep, exercise, and nutrition plays a pivotal role in supporting the body's healing process. Holistic methods expand to include additional therapies like Ayurveda, acupuncture, yoga, meditation, music therapy, and massage therapy to enhance overall health and alleviate physical issues.

Holistic medicine and nursing consider the psychological, physical, social, and spiritual needs of patients. Providing holistic care proves effective in enhancing the well-being of cancer patients.

Amidst the rollercoaster of emotions cancer patients experience from fear to hope, anxiety to depression, frustration to anger, and moments of resilience coping with uncertainty and treatment side effects becomes paramount.

Holistic treatment doesn't solely focus on the body itself, but it also addresses emotions through support groups, counselling, and mindfulness exercises, fostering emotional well-being and a positive mindset which are crucial to the healing process.

Exploring the mind is a complex and multifaceted aspect of human consciousness and cognition. It encompasses various mental processes such as thoughts, emotions, perceptions, memories, beliefs, and intentions. The mind is responsible for our ability to think, reason, feel, and make decisions. It plays a crucial role in shaping our perceptions of the world and how we interact with it.

From a psychological perspective, the mind can be divided into different levels or components, including the conscious mind involving thoughts and perceptions that we are aware of, and the subconscious mind, which consists of underlying beliefs, attitudes, and automatic processes that influence our behaviour without conscious awareness.

The mind is also closely connected to the brain, the physical organ responsible for processing information and generating thoughts and emotions. While the brain provides the biological substrate for mental processes, the mind encompasses the subjective experience and interpretation of those processes.

Throughout history, various philosophical, psychological, and scientific perspectives have sought to understand the nature of the mind and its relationship to the body and the external world. This exploration has led to the development of fields such as cognitive psychology, neuroscience, and consciousness studies, which continue to investigate the mysteries of the mind and its profound impact on human experience and behavior.

Spirituality often overlooked in traditional medical care, holds significance in holistic cancer care. It goes beyond religion, encompassing finding meaning and connection to something larger. Spiritual support provides comfort and strength, easing and soothing the understanding and experience of the cancer journey.

Taking charge and openly discussing needs is pivotal in holistic care. Actively learning about treatment options, sharing concerns, and participating in decisions empowers patients reinforcing the idea that each person is valuable as a whole.

In essence, understanding cancer holistically means looking beyond medicine and conventional treatment recognizing the interconnectedness of body, mind, and spirit. But not to overlook conventional medical treatment. Embracing this dual approach empowers those facing cancer to boost resilience, improve life, and follow a path to recovery that addresses all aspects of their well-being.

Also combining ayurveda with conventional cancer treatment forms a holistic approach. While conventional methods target cancer directly, ayurveda focuses on balancing the body through personalized practices like diet, herbs, yoga, meditation, and stress management. This complementary approach aims to support overall well-being during treatment, but it's essential to consult both oncologists and Ayurvedic practitioners for a coordinated and safe strategy. Ayurveda enhances the body's natural healing alongside evidence-based medical interventions.

Optimal cancer care necessitates a dual approach, integrating conventional treatments with holistic methods. While holistic approaches offer valuable support, relying solely on them risks compromising proven medical interventions. A synergistic strategy, combining evidence-based treatments and holistic practices, ensures a comprehensive and personalized approach to cancer management, enhancing both direct targeting of the disease and overall patient well-being.

Perception Shapes Reality

"Transforming **Perceptions** and Cultivating Resilience in the Face of Adversity"

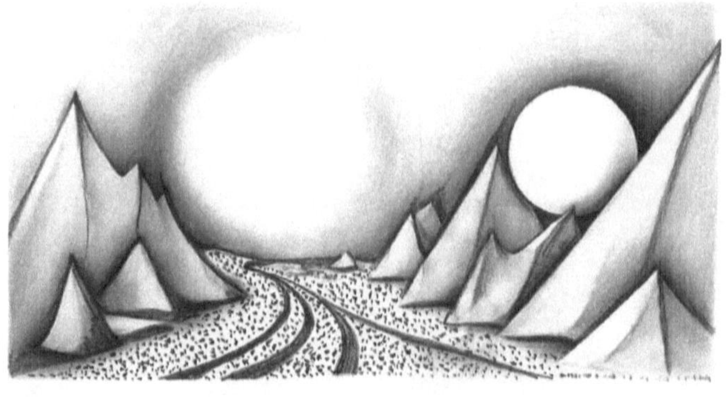

"Cancer's journey a rhythm to find, perception's melody shapes the mind and paints the portrait one of its kinds."

Understanding cancer extends beyond its medical dimensions, delving into the intricate interplay of emotions, thoughts, and societal influences that shape individuals' experiences with the disease. Initially fear and uncertainty often prevail influenced by cultural beliefs, personal experiences, and societal stigmas. These emotions transform an individual's progress through their cancer journey.

Perception emerges as a pivotal factor in how people confront and face cancer, make treatment decisions, and maintain overall well-being. Positive perceptions empower individuals to face their diagnosis with resilience, viewing challenges as opportunities for personal growth. Conversely, negative perceptions cast a shadow on the journey affecting emotional well-being and the ability to navigate the complexities of treatment.

Supporting individuals in comprehending the personal nature of their perceptions is vital. Encouraging open communication, addressing misunderstandings, and promoting awareness contribute to a more informed and empowered perception of cancer. Recognizing diverse perceptions fosters empathy and supports a holistic approach to cancer care and its treatments.

For cancer patients, the power of perception significantly shapes their journey influencing their understanding of reality and practicality. Amid the challenges of a cancer diagnosis, subjective interpretation becomes a fundamental aspect of the human experience. Mental models act as filters impacting how patients perceive their situation and reality.

Encouraging patients to understand the power of their perception is a call to mindfulness and awareness. By recognizing subjectivity they can question assumptions, broaden perspectives, and foster empowerment. This awareness facilitates empathy acknowledging that each patient navigates their cancer journey differently based on their unique experiences.

Present views posit that cancer alters our perspective, urging us to find strength in vulnerability and recognize might in frailty. It emphasizes finding hope in uncertainty and the beauty of resilience in the face of adversity. In conclusion, the dynamic relationship between perception and reality significantly shapes the experience of cancer patients.

Embracing the power of perception allows individuals to navigate through their journey with awareness, resilience, and appreciation for diverse perspectives within the cancer community. The transformative lens of the power of perception in the cancer journey turns challenges into opportunities, resilience into strength, and the human spirit into a beacon of hope.

In simpler terms understanding cancer involves more than just the medical side. People's feelings and thoughts along with societal influences shape how they experience the disease. Initially, there's often fear but these feelings change as individuals go through and experience their cancer journey.

Perception or how people see and understand things is crucial in how they cope with cancer and make treatment decisions. For instance, a person might perceive their cancer diagnosis as a wake-up call to prioritize health leading to positive lifestyle changes and a newfound appreciation for life's moments. Positive perceptions help individuals face their diagnosis with strength, viewing challenges as chances to recover and grow. On the other hand, negative perceptions can make the journey harder affecting emotions and the ability to deal with treatment throughout the journey.

It's important to help individuals understand that how they see things is personal and can change. Talking openly and clearly, addressing misunderstandings and miscommunication, and spreading awareness all help create a more informed and empowered view of cancer and its treatments. Recognizing that everyone sees things differently promotes empathy and a well-rounded approach to cancer care.

For cancer patients how they perceive their situation shapes their journey. Even though cancer is tough, how patients interpret it becomes a big part of their experience. Encouraging patients to understand the power of their perception, means being mindful and aware. Recognizing that each person's journey is unique and being open to different perspectives helps build empathy and resilience.

This view highlights that cancer changes how we see things, pushing us to find strength in vulnerability and see power in the fragile. It encourages finding hope in uncertain times and appreciating resilience in tough situations.

In conclusion how people perceive cancer significantly affects their experience in the long journey. By embracing the power of perception individuals can navigate their journey with awareness, strength, and an understanding of different perspectives within the cancer community and their circle. This view suggests that looking at cancer from a different angle turns challenges into chances to grow resilience into strength and the human spirit into a source of hope and recovery.

Ultimately a collective effort involving medical professionals, support systems, caretakers, educational resources and a positive cultural environment contributes to changing the perception of an individual in the cancer journey

Fostering Resilience

"Nurturing strength through **mindset**"

"Through treatments and trials, each hurdle we face, Embrace a positive mindset which gives us strength and grace."

Cancer, a word laden with fear and despair impacts millions worldwide, altering lives in profound ways. The mindset with which a person approaches their diagnosis, treatment, and recovery can have a profound impact on their overall well-being and outlook on life. Cancer treatments can be gruelling and physically demanding, often leaving individuals feeling exhausted and emotionally drained. Lack of resilience can make you feel helpless and stuck to cope with the situation, however, amidst the challenges, a ray of hope emerges – **The power of mindset**.

Having a positive mindset characterized by hope, determination, and belief in inner strength, can significantly make you resilient which influences the journey of cancer. The patient's mindset also plays a pivotal role in embracing a holistic approach to treatment. Cancer treatments involve medical interventions and lifestyle changes. A positive mindset enables patients to approach these changes with determination, viewing them as opportunities for growth and healing, rather than inconveniences.

The role of mindset is not to be underestimated extending beyond a mere coping mechanism. It's firmly believed that a positive mindset enhances a patient's ability to cope with tough situations and combat cancer. It contributes to improved quality of life making him more resilient and may even enhance chances of recovery with survival.

Harnessing a resilient mindset doesn't make your problems disappear; instead makes you better and stronger to handle them. It keeps you keep going. Being resilient can help you overcome psychological conditions such as fear, anxiety, and depression which can contribute to overall mental health being.

Talking to your mental healthcare professional would be helpful to achieve a resilient mindset and mental wellness in the journey of cancer.

Maintaining hope and being more optimistic is a cornerstone of a positive mindset in the face of the uncertainties and hurdles that accompany cancer. This mindset proves crucial during the arduous battle keeping patients motivated and focused on their treatment. The impact extends to physical well-being with positive emotions strengthening the immune system and supporting the body's natural defence mechanism. Having **hope** allows individuals to envision a future beyond cancer set goals and aspirations and stay motivated during treatment. It serves as a beacon of light in the darkest of times providing strength and purpose to go.

Determination is a quality often seen in individuals who successfully navigate the challenges of cancer. This mindset involves a strong will to persevere to fight against all odds and not let the disease define or limit one's potential power. It is the power of determination that keeps individuals going even in the face of adversity and odds. Believing in one's inner strength is a mindset that can propel individuals forward in their cancer journey. It is the belief that they have what it takes to overcome the challenges to heal and lead a fulfilling life beyond the illness. This mindset empowers individuals to take an active role in their treatment to make positive lifestyle changes and to advocate for their well-being.

To improve your **resilience** you should take action every time from lessons learnt from experience. Keeping you present in the movement and making every day meaningful.

The support and care of loved ones become integral in nurturing a positive mindset. Encouragement, love, and understanding create a supportive environment uplifting the patient's spirits. It's important to recognize and harness the power of mindset to create a supportive and uplifting atmosphere.

"You have got fantastic Resilience beyond measure! Your resilience requires a standing ovulation"

Above encouraging words by supporting groups can make you uplift your resilience to cope with hurdles in the path of cancer.

In other words, the transformative power of mindset in the cancer journey is undeniable. A positive mindset provides hope, improves well-being, and enhances a patient's ability to navigate the challenges of the disease. Encourages both patients and their loved ones to embrace and leverage the strength of mindset facing the journey with **courage, resilience, hope, and determination.**

Breathe of Resilience

Navigating life's challenges with strength of Breathe.

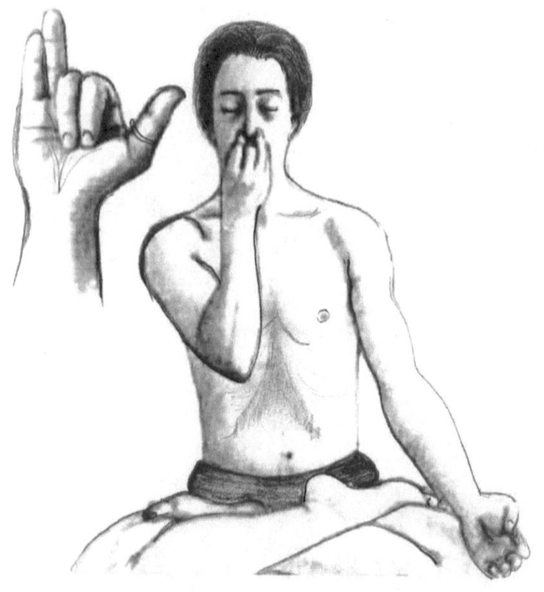

"In life's space of strife, a breath of resilience is our sweet song. A melody of strength with each breath, we rise and stand, striving in a symphony of courage hand in hand, with resilience so grand."

Individuals on a cancer journey often face specific breathing challenges such as labored breathing, and chest tightness experienced by cancer patients. Dyspnea (shortness of breath) due to factors such as pleural effusion (fluid trapped in lungs), inflammation, surgeries, chemotherapy, radiation, tumours in lungs, and weakened lung muscles, certain cancer treatments may contribute to respiratory issues as side effects

Cancer patients can evoke a range of emotional responses including stress, anxiety, and depression, which can further impact breathing patterns leading to shallow and rapid breathing. It's essential to acknowledge and address these feelings and implement breathing exercises under the guidance of a health care provider.

Managing breathlessness is crucial which affects daily activities and sleep. While breathing is automatic, being conscious of it can improve overall well-being. Tailored breathing and holistic techniques such as mindful breathing, box breathing, and the 4-7-8 technique may strengthen lung muscles and enhance respiration. Consult healthcare providers before starting any breathing exercises and choose techniques suitable for individual needs. A comprehensive rehabilitation program and practicing alternate therapy such as yoga, meditation, and chiropractic with conventional treatment under the guidance of professionals may be beneficial to ease breathing.

Incorporate foods that have anti-inflammatory action for your lungs such as turmeric, ginger, green tea, and foods containing omega-3 fatty acids.

Addressing underlying causes such as anxiety and fatigue through relaxation and psychotherapy can alleviate symptoms promoting overall well-being during the cancer journey. Regular check-ins with healthcare providers ensures a tailored approach to managing both physical and emotional aspects of breathing challenges in the context of cancer.

Harmony of Emotions

Crafting harmony between emotions and
feelings for a fulfilling life.

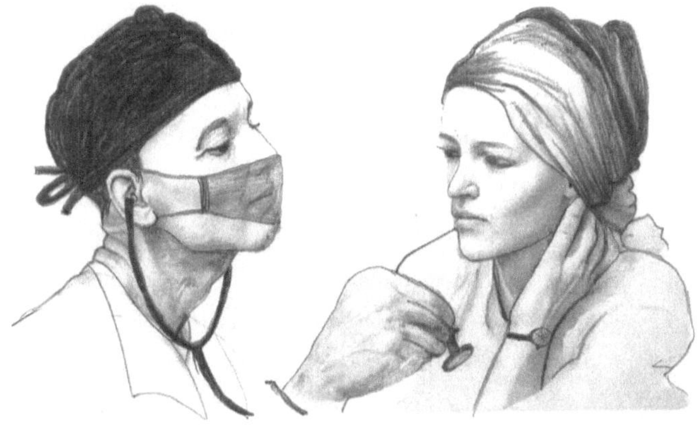

*"In the realm of cancer's emotion, resilience is the potion.
Tears may flow, fears may show, but hope blooms in the
shadows always glow."*

Receiving a cancer diagnosis can be a significant shock, triggering a mix of emotions. Feeling scared, surprised, and unsure is common, and also raises anxiety about the future and treatment. It's crucial to talk to friends your family and doctors for support and guidance during this emotional time.

Healthcare providers, including oncology social workers, psychologists, and psychiatrists play key roles in addressing a range of emotions including sadness, anger, and frustration as they navigate through diagnosis, treatment, and recovery during the cancer journey. They provide support and collaborate with the oncology team to ensure comprehensive care offering counselling to help individuals cope with the emotions that impact the diagnosis. Coping with the loss of normalcy, and plans, and sometimes the loss of relationships can be emotionally taxing. The financial burden of medical bills and the impact on one's ability to work can contribute to emotional distress.

Psychosocial impacts, such as changes in physical appearances, such as hair loss, mastectomy (removal of breasts), ostomy, and having a colostomy bag after colorectal cancer surgery and many such may affect their intimate relationship as well as self-esteem, which can lead to feeling of isolation or dependency.

Cancer is not just an individual struggle. Coping with a loved one's cancer diagnosis is tough and tedious; it presents profound emotional challenges for family members. Fear of the unknown, loss, and the future can create anxiety. Feeling helpless is common as you watch your loved ones going through treatment and are unable to control the situation. Sadness and grief become constant companions as normal life is disrupted and disturbed.

Communication within the family can be strained, but openly discussing fears and concerns is crucial for unity. Balancing care giving and daily life is challenging, leading to emotional exhaustion and stress. Seeking professional support from support groups like social workers, counsellors or psychologists is essential for expressing feelings and gaining coping strategies, additionally, it also offers a sense of community and understanding.

Emotional well-being is essential for overall health. Understanding and expressing feelings genuinely, coupled with emotional intelligence play vital roles in navigating the emotional challenges of a cancer diagnosis. High emotional intelligence helps individuals cope with fear and anxiety, fostering empathetic interactions and resilience throughout the cancer journey.

Expressing emotions honestly, whether through talking, art or physical activities is crucial in coping with the challenges of cancer. Sharing feelings, engaging in creative pursuits, and participating in activities that bring joy contribute to mental well-being. Being aware of feelings without judgment is key to staying emotionally healthy, and finding effective coping mechanisms such as support and mindfulness which helps deal with life's ups and downs.

Taking care of emotional well-being not only benefits mental health but also strengthens relationships and community. It involves recognizing and expressing emotions openly, contributing to a positive mindset during the journey of cancer.

In conclusion, both cancer patients as well as family members of a patient going through cancer are involved in navigating their fears, helplessness, and sadness. Effective communication within the family and seeking professional support play crucial roles in supporting each other through the emotional challenges of the cancer journey.

Radiant Minds

Cultivating **Positivity** and Overcoming
Negativity in Cancer.

"Positivity is the way to transform shadows into beams of day. Though negativity may try to pull us down, with hope in our hearts, we wear successful crown."

Promoting and weaving threads of **optimism** through positive affirmations fortifies the mind and helps challenge and limit negative thoughts and emotions. It is a vital tool to cultivate a resilient mindset in challenging situations while facing cancer.

It is seen that patients with low levels of optimism are at greater risk of experiencing mental distress and require greater psychosocial support. Strengthening an optimistic attitude may be an effective tool for supporting patients in adapting to their disease.

Maintaining a characteristic positive attitude and being away from a pessimistic attitude can make you resilient, and strengthen you with positivity and courage in your journey through cancer.

Dealing with a cancer diagnosis and undergoing treatment can be incredibly challenging, bringing about major life stressors. Negative thoughts may creep in, replaying distressing moments from the past or causing worry about the unknown future. While **distractions** can sometimes help persistent negative thoughts may lead to feelings of helplessness, self-loathing, or anger, potentially escalating into clinical depression.

To manage these repetitive negative thoughts, it's essential to identify their source. Seeking self-awareness through counselling can facilitate the process of self-discovery, transforming self-defeating thoughts into life-affirming ones.

Counting blessings, regardless of their size, daily can expand the mind and shift a negative perspective.

Engaging in positive self-talk is another powerful strategy. Replace negative thoughts with empowering statements, mantras, or prayers, repeating them while consciously breathing to release anxieties. Drawing strength from inspirational stories of cancer survivors can encourage during challenging moments. Remind yourself continually that you can not only survive but thrive.

Staying in the present moment is crucial. Through deep breathing and meditation, cultivate awareness and mindfulness of thoughts, feelings, and experiences. This practice helps embrace the present experience, fostering resilience and reducing reactivity.

Recognizing what you can and cannot control is key. Worrying about uncontrollable aspects may impede recovery due to increased stress hormones. Schedule dedicated time, around 20 to 30 minutes a day to address worries and free you from anxious thoughts at other times. For matters within your control, outline goals and steps to fulfil them.

Viewing mistakes as learning opportunities is fundamental. Rather than reacting with regret or anger, perceive mistakes as lessons that guide you to do things differently and better. When emotionally ready, share your experiences with fellow cancer patients to encourage and grow in compassion towards yourself and others.

Remember, seeking help is perfectly okay. If overwhelming feelings affect your daily routines, consider talking to a mental health professional like a counsellor. You're not alone in reaching out for support, surround yourself with knowledge, and remember that seeking help is strength in itself.

Gratitude & Giggles

"Nurturing **Joy** amidst Challenges"

"In the rhythm of life's song, let laughter dance and gratitude sing, for in their melody, cancer's shadows lose and break their string."

The Transformative Power of Gratitude Journaling and the Alleviation of Life's Challenges through Maintaining a Sense of **Humour**

In the pursuit of holistic well-being, individuals often find solace and empowerment in two seemingly disparate practices: gratitude journaling and maintaining a sense of humour, as one said laughter is a great medicine. Exploring the profound impact of these practices on mental and emotional states, as well as their potential to navigate life's challenges with resilience and positivity.

Gratitude journaling involves the deliberate act of reflecting on and documenting the positive aspects of one's life. This practice has been associated with numerous mental health benefits, including increased life satisfaction, improved mood, and reduced stress levels. By acknowledging and appreciating the small moments of joy, individuals can cultivate a mindset that focuses on the positive aspects of their experiences. Gratitude journaling serves as a daily reminder of the abundance of positive elements in one's life, fostering a sense of contentment and resilience in the face of adversity.

- Express gratitude for getting a chance to wake up to a new day, embracing the opportunity for healing and potential for growth is a transformative journey.

- Acknowledge the strength you received within to face challenges with resilience.

- Reflect on the beauty of nature, whether it's a sunrise or sunset, a gentle breeze of air, or the soothing sound of rain.

- Be thankful and grateful for those who present you with the small moments that bring peace and joy during the cancer journey.

- List and prioritize individuals who have been pillars of support from family, friends, and healthcare providers.

- Appreciate the love, understanding, and encouragement received on this challenging path.

- Acknowledge the body's resilience and its ability to heal.

- Express gratitude for moments of strength and progress in the healing process. no matter how small the step is

- Note acts of kindness received, whether from loved ones, strangers, or healthcare professionals.

- Recognize and appreciate the compassion and care that make the cancer journey more bearable.

- Celebrate milestones no matter how minor they are in the treatment and recovery process.

- Express gratitude for the progress made and the lessons learned along the way.

- Recall moments of laughter, joy, or simple pleasures experienced.

- Express gratitude for these moments that uplift the spirit and provide a reprieve from the challenges.

- Reflect on personal strengths and resilience.

- Appreciate the ability to adapt, learn, and find moments of peace within oneself.

- Recognize the dedication and expertise of the healthcare team.

- Express gratitude for their support, guidance, and commitment to the well-being of the patient.

- Before bedtime, express thanks for the day's experiences, challenges, and the opportunity for growth.

- Reflect on the positive aspects, reinforcing a mindset of gratitude even in difficult times.

Not to forget this gratitude journal is a personal space for reflection and acknowledgment. Tailor each entry to your own experiences and allow it to be a source of positivity and hope on your cancer journey.

Humour and laughter have long been recognized as a powerful coping mechanism in the face of life's challenges. Maintaining a sense of humour involves finding lightness and amusement even in difficult and painful situations. This practice is not about dismissing the seriousness of life but rather about approaching challenges with a perspective that allows for resilience and emotional balance. Humour can act as a natural stress reliever, promoting a positive outlook and facilitating better problem-solving skills. It fosters a mindset that embraces imperfections and sees opportunities for growth even in adversity.

The combination of gratitude journaling and maintaining a sense of humor creates a powerful synergy. Gratitude provides a foundation of positivity allowing individuals to navigate challenges with a mindset focused on solutions and opportunities rather than obstacles. Meanwhile, humour implements lightness into the journey, acting as a counterbalance to the weight of life's difficulties. Together these practices contribute to a more resilient and optimistic approach to daily in life.

Incorporating gratitude journaling and humour into daily routines requires commitment and intentionality Creating a daily habit of jotting down moments of gratitude and finding reasons to laugh, whether through shared jokes, humorous perspectives, or engaging in activities that bring joy, which can significantly enhance mental mood and emotional well-being.

By consciously embracing gratitude and humour, individuals equip themselves with invaluable tools to face life's uncertainties with grace and strength. These practices not only enhance personal well-being but also contribute to the cultivation of a positive and supportive environment, as individuals embark on the journey of gratitude journaling and maintaining a sense of humour, they open doors to a more resilient, joyful, and fulfilling existence.

Soulful Support

"Nurturing psychological well-being in the cancer journey is akin to extending a soulful support, a compassionate embrace through every step."

"Going through the valley of uncertainty and nightmare, may the wings of support lift you and the gentle hands guide you with compassion and care"

Support is foundational in the journey of those facing cancer, reaching out to both patients and their caregivers. Encouraging individuals dealing with cancer to seek psychological support is paramount. Professionals including counsellors, therapists, and support groups offer invaluable assistance in navigating the emotional labyrinth that accompanies a cancer diagnosis.

In this expedition, caregivers emerge as linchpins, orchestrating emotional support, assisting with daily tasks, and advocating for patients. Juggling responsibilities from managing medication to gathering information about the diagnosis from time to time. Caregivers also play a crucial role in facilitating communication within the healthcare team. Simultaneously, they navigate financial matters and logistics, all while prioritizing their self-care to effectively bolster the patient.

It's important to maintain faith in healthcare providers which is at most crucial. Their commitment to treating everyone without discrimination based on caste, religion, social status, or financial standing is a cornerstone of ethical and compassionate healthcare

Caregivers form a diverse tapestry—family members, friends, partners, or professional caregivers like nurses are all bound by their compassion and reliability. Family support stands out, not just for its practical contributions but for its emotional fortitude, profoundly aiding those grappling with cancer and enriching overall well-being. The love and unwavering commitment of these loved ones create a resilient network providing a foundation of strength for both patients and caregivers alike.

The care giving tableau often comprises a collaborative effort, where a combination of individuals shares responsibilities. The crux lies in ensuring that these caregivers possess the capability to meet the diverse needs of the person battling cancer.

Holistic therapies, such as yoga, meditation, or art therapy assume a pivotal role in promoting mental well-being for cancer patients. Caregivers including loved ones become champions of these activities, integrating them seamlessly into the holistic approach to care.

Communication, an art between caregivers and patients, becomes paramount. Active listening and open dialogue create a supportive environment, addressing emotional needs and concerns. Equally crucial is respite care, acknowledging the caregiver's need for breaks to prevent burnout and preserve their well-being.

Expanding the support network, caregivers along with loved ones tap into community resources, linking with local support organizations. Technology serves as a connector, bridging patients and caregivers with online communities, support forums, and virtual resources.

Navigating through cancer treatment presents many challenges impacting not just the patient but also placing a substantial burden on the caregiver and support groups. Maintaining unwavering optimism during the prolonged and draining journey is pivotal, nurturing strength and solidarity until the conclusion. Cancer treatment is a challenging journey, not only for the patient but also for the caregiver. Sustaining high morale throughout the lengthy and exhausting process is crucial for both, fostering resilience and support until the end

Coping strategies unfold as additional tools such as mindfulness techniques, journaling, or engaging in hobbies. The social support narrative woven into a holistic approach to care aligns emotional, practical, and social elements, which offer a compass for improved outcomes and an enriched quality of life amid the challenges of cancer.

Support groups, and caregivers should send heartfelt words of motivation, encouragement, and admiration to lift the spirits during this challenging journey. Such as:

You are facing cancer with a remarkable smile – truly impressive!

Navigating the challenges of the cancer battle with style – well done!

Your resilience deserves a standing ovation – applause!

Turning the seriousness of cancer into a comedy roast – you're a humour hero!

Guiding through the cancer journey with a dose of laughter – legendary!

Confronting cancer with a sense of humour – brilliant!

Your laughter is a healing balm – prescription-approved!

Facing cancer with grace and style – fabulous!

You're not just overcoming cancer; you're winning the humour game – hilarious!

Responding to cancer with epic laughter – pure genius!

You're making a superhero impact in the care giving world!

Your care giving skills are as sharp as ninja moves!

Infusing care giving with a sprinkle of laughter – you're a pro!

An extraordinary caregiver – making tough days more bearable!

Your humour is a secret weapon in the care giving arsenal!

Juggling care giving tasks like a circus master – hats off!

Transforming care giving into a comedy – you've mastered the art!

Your humour is medicine for both the patient and yourself!

You've mastered the care giving humour game – a true comedian!

Navigating the care giving rollercoaster with a side of laughter – brilliant!

Providing incredible support!

Your dedication is truly extraordinary!

You stand as a pillar of strength!

Remarkable care giving in every aspect!

Your commitment is unwavering!

Your compassion knows no bounds!

A true beacon of comfort!

Your selflessness is truly inspiring!

Thank you for your tireless care!

You're making a significant and positive difference!

Enduring with grace and resilience!

Your strength is truly awe-inspiring!

Pushing through the challenges like a true champion!

Resilience beyond measure!

Bearing it all with incredible fortitude!

You're a living testament to perseverance!

Rising above the pain with incredible spirit!

Your determination is truly powerful!

Facing the challenges with remarkable resilience!

Unbelievably strong!

A powerhouse of courage!

Exceptional tenacity!

An inspiration beyond words!

An unwavering spirit!

Formidable!

Truly a force to be reckoned with!

Unstoppable determination!

Exemplary strength!

Unparalleled bravery!

Outstanding effort!

Brilliant!

You're a true inspiration!

Magnificent!

Way to go!

You're unstoppable!

Fantastic resilience!

You're a rock star!

Impressive!

You're showing tremendous bravery!

Absolutely! You're a warrior!

Fantastic job!

You're a beacon of strength!

Remarkable!

Keep pushing forward!

You're doing incredible!

Marvellous!

You're a true hero!

Outstanding!

You've got tremendous courage!

Absolutely!

You've got this!

Keep shining!

You are resilient!

Bravo!

Stay strong!

Incredible!

You inspire us!

You're a fighter!

Amazing!

In this journey marked by resilience and collaboration, caregivers loved ones, and patients together paint a portrait of unwavering support that transcends the confines of diagnosis and treatment, embracing the human spirit with empathy and strength. The tapestry of care, woven with compassion and understanding, fortifies individuals against the challenges, creating a sanctuary of support that not only endures but blossoms through every chapter of the cancer journey.

Moreover, the role of psychologists becomes pivotal in this intricate tapestry. When required, these professionals contribute their expertise, offering tailored psychological support to both patients and caregivers. Their insights help navigate the complex emotional terrain, providing coping mechanisms and strategies for maintaining mental well-being. The psychologist, as a crucial member of the support network, further enhances the comprehensive care provided in the journey of cancer, ensuring that emotional resilience remains a cornerstone of the entire experience.

Various countries have come up with supportive helplines which have emerged as beacons of assistance to ease the emotional burden for those navigating the tumultuous cancer journey. Cancer help lines are like always-available friends who understand that tough times don't follow a schedule. Day or night, even on holidays, they're there to listen and offer a compassionate ear for anyone dealing with cancer.

Staffed by trained professionals, these helplines provide emotional support helping patients express fears and uncertainties without judgment. They're experts in navigating the emotional ups and downs that come with a cancer diagnosis.

These helplines go beyond just listening. They also offer practical information on treatments, managing side effects, and coping strategies. So that patients not only get emotional support but also gain valuable insights into their medical journey, helping them make informed decisions.

For those hesitant to share feelings with friends or family, helplines provide a confidential and judgment-free space. This anonymity encourages open communication and helps individuals confront and process their emotions without worrying about loved ones.

Thanks to technology, many helplines now offer online chat services, making emotional support accessible to those who prefer digital communication. This adaptability ensures that people from different backgrounds and preferences can benefit from these helplines.

In a nutshell, cancer helps lines play a crucial role in providing emotional support for patients. They're like constant pillars of strength, offering support, professional guidance, and confidential space for anyone facing the emotional challenges of cancer. In tough times, these helplines stand as powerful allies, providing reassurance and a sense of community for those on the challenging journey of cancer.

One-on-one sessions with a trained counsellor or therapist who can provide emotional support, and coping strategies, and help address specific concerns related to the cancer diagnosis and treatment. Group counselling sessions bring together individuals with cancer, survivors, and caregivers to share experiences, provide mutual support, and learn coping skills from one another. Counselling sessions are specifically designed for couples affected by cancer, focusing on communication, relationship dynamics, intimacy issues, and coping strategies to navigate the challenges together. Counselling sessions involving family members of individuals with cancer to address family dynamics, and communication patterns, and provide support to both the patient and their loved ones. Counselling sessions for individuals and families who are grieving the loss of a loved one to cancer, helping them navigate the grieving process, cope with loss, and find ways to honour and remember their loved one. Counselling that addresses the psychological, social, and emotional aspects of cancer, including stress management, anxiety, depression, body image concerns, and adjustment to life changes following a cancer diagnosis. Counselling is provided by trained professionals to individuals and families with a history of cancer, focusing on assessing cancer risk, understanding genetic testing results, and making informed decisions about prevention and screening options.

These approaches can be tailored to meet the specific needs and preferences of individuals and families affected by cancer, providing valuable support and resources throughout the cancer journey.

Self-Care Symphony

Nurturing the Self.

"Navigate the depths & conquer the night make yourself a guiding light".

Facing a cancer diagnosis is a profound and challenging experience that not only impacts the physical body but also takes a toll on one's mental and emotional well-being. In such a journey, prioritizing self-care, self-empowerment, self-compassion, and awareness becomes imperative in your Cancer Path which involves being kind to yourself. These elements serve as guiding beacons offering strength and resilience amid the storm of uncertainty.

At the core of navigating the cancer path is self-care, a practice that involves nurturing the body, mind, and soul. This encompasses adhering to medical treatments, adopting a balanced diet, engaging in regular exercise, and ensuring adequate rest. Beyond the physical aspect, self-care extends to cultivating a positive mindset, seeking emotional support, and indulging in activities that bring joy. Recognizing the symbiotic relationship between physical and mental health is vital for a holistic approach to well-being.

Take time to make decisions about how we care for ourselves. Indulge in activities that soothe your mind, body, and soul. Figure out what's right for you.

Some activities such as aromatherapy, massage, art therapy, cooking, and spending time with loved ones might take out your stress and relax your mind and body. Being kind to yourself and learning to love yourself is a heart of self-care.

In the face of adversity, self-empowerment emerges as a potent tool for individuals grappling with cancer. This involves taking an active role in decision-making regarding treatment plans, being informed about one's condition, and fostering a sense of control over aspects of life that can be managed. Empowerment is not only about asserting agency but also about embracing the ability to adapt and find meaning amid challenges. It transforms the narrative from victimhood to resilience, instilling a sense of strength that propels individuals forward.

Amid the whirlwind of medical appointments, treatments, and emotional upheavals, self-compassion acts as a gentle anchor. Acknowledging and accepting one's vulnerabilities, fears, and limitations, foster a kinder relationship with oneself. Instead of self-judgment, compassion allows individuals to embrace their humanity and navigate the uncertainties of the cancer journey with grace. It involves extending the same kindness and understanding to oneself as one would to a close friend, cultivating emotional resilience in challenging situations. Cancer, with its myriad challenges, prompts a profound shift in self-awareness both of oneself and the world. It involves being attuned to the body's signals, understanding the importance of mental well-being, and recognizing the value of every moment. Awareness also extends beyond the individual, encompassing a broader understanding of the support systems available, the significance of advocacy, and the importance of contributing to the collective knowledge about cancer. Informed awareness empowers individuals to make decisions aligned with their values and aspirations.

In Conclusion prioritizing self-care, self-empowerment, self-compassion and awareness on the cancer path is akin to tending to a delicate garden amid a storm. Each element plays a crucial role in nurturing resilience, fostering a positive mindset, and embracing the journey with a sense of purpose. As individuals embark on this challenging expedition, they find within themselves the capacity to not just endure, but to flourish and inspire others along the way. In the face of adversity, the light of self-care, self-empowerment, self-compassion, and awareness illuminate the path towards healing and transformation.

Empowerment in Action

--—∞—--

"Empowering Journeys of Cancer through
Communication and Self-Advocacy"

*"In the cancer maze, let's embrace self-advocacy to find the
strength to face, and communication pave the way towards
healing and grace"*

In the journey of cancer, you are the only one taking charge of your health. Acknowledging and learning about your illness in depth and treatment options, Involving yourself or actively participating in your health care decision.

Open **communication** with your doctor and healthcare provider is a must. If necessary, advocate for a second opinion and ensure your concerns are addressed. Ask questions, and express your preferences.

Your voice and input are crucial in guiding and shaping your cancer journey ensuring personalized, informed care, and getting the care that's right for you. A second opinion in cancer involves consulting with another doctor to confirm the diagnosis or explore different treatment options. It can provide reassurance for your specific situation.

Establishing open lines of communication fosters understanding, and helps in decision-making. Effective communication in cancer is vital for both patients and their support networks. Involve sharing feelings and information and clearly express your needs and preferences.

To minimize the risk of misinterpretation, ensure all medical records and test results are accurately shared between the original and second-opinion doctor.

In the challenging journey of cancer, effective communication and self-advocacy are crucial pillars of support for individuals facing this formidable battle.

Cancer not only impacts physical health but also takes a toll on emotional well-being, underscoring the importance of clear communication and self-advocacy in navigating the complexities of diagnosis and treatment.

Enrolling in a cancer clinical trial demands careful consideration. Begin by fully understanding the trial details, discussing personal goals with your healthcare provider, and asking questions to clarify any uncertainties. Seek a second opinion, especially if needed, to ensure the trial aligns with your situation. Understand the financial aspects, involve your support system, and evaluate eligibility criteria. Explore alternative options, assess emotional readiness, and review the informed consent document thoroughly. This proactive and collaborative approach empowers you to make well-informed decisions before embarking on a clinical trial journey

Communication plays a pivotal role in connecting individuals with healthcare professionals. Open and honest dialogue with doctors and nurses is essential for understanding the diagnosis, treatment options, and potential side effects. This communication empowers patients to make informed decisions about their healthcare, actively participate in their treatment plans, and ensures that any concerns or questions are addressed promptly, leading to improved outcomes and satisfaction.

Equally vital is communication with family and friends forming a strong support network. Honest discussions about feelings, fears, and concerns create a safe space for emotional expression, reducing anxiety and stress. This open communication not only strengthens the support system around the patient but also plays a crucial role in their psychological well-being.

Furthermore, communication extends to the broader cancer community. Connecting with others who have experienced or are currently undergoing cancer provides comfort and empathy. Shared experiences, advice, and coping strategies that empower patients and help them navigate the challenges of cancer. The advent of technology has further facilitated communication through online support groups, social media, and online medicine, breaking down geographical barriers and providing convenience.

In parallel, **self-advocacy** becomes a beacon of empowerment in the cancer journey. It refers to the ability of individuals to speak up for themselves, express their needs, and actively participate in their healthcare decisions. Being well-informed is a cornerstone of self-advocacy, involving education about the disease, treatment options, and potential side effects. This knowledge empowers individuals to ask the right questions, make informed decisions and actively engage with their healthcare team.

Building a strong support network is another dimension of self-advocacy, encompassing not only the healthcare team but also family, friends, and cancer support groups. This support network provides emotional strength and practical assistance creating a community that understands and empathizes with the challenges faced by cancer patients.

Communication skills play a pivotal role in self-advocacy. Open and honest communication with healthcare professionals about concerns, fears, and preferences encourages a collaborative approach to treatment.

Taking personal responsibility for our health is crucial. While many external factors can contribute to diseases like cancer, such as environmental pollutants, genetics, and lifestyle factors, we can still take proactive steps to minimize our risks. This includes maintaining a healthy diet, exercising regularly, avoiding harmful substances like tobacco and excessive alcohol, getting regular check-ups, and managing stress effectively. By focusing on what we can control, we empower ourselves to lead healthier lives despite the challenges posed by external factors.

Being proactive about managing physical and emotional well-being is also part of self-advocacy, involving adherence to treatment regimens, adopting a healthy lifestyle, and seeking help for emotional support and counselling.

In some cases where cancer patients are unable to communicate or advocate for themselves during their treatment, it's essential for their support system, including family, friends, or healthcare professionals to actively engage in understanding their needs, preferences, and treatment goals. Collaborate closely with the medical team to ensure the best possible care and quality of life for the individual.

In conclusion, effective communication and self-advocacy are integral aspects of the cancer journey. They empower individuals to actively participate in their treatment processes, make informed decisions, and build a robust support system. As technology advances and dialogue continues to be encouraged, we can create a more supportive and informed environment for cancer patients.

Navigating Life's Challenges

Understanding and adapting to Adversity and embracing flexibility.

"Twist and turn, the lesson to be learned, challenges to be faced in every pace, through trail and tests, our resilience is earned, in the dance of life, we navigate the maze"

Facing cancer involves grappling with challenges like feeling unwell, emotional stress, and financial concerns. Adapting to this adversity means dealing with the uncertainties that come with cancer, and being open to adjusting plans and thoughts during treatment and recovery.

Cancer, with its physical, emotional, and financial toll, presents a formidable challenge. Adapting to this adversity involves acknowledging changes and finding ways to navigate them. For example, someone undergoing cancer treatment might face unexpected side effects, requiring flexibility to manage these challenges and seek support when needed.

Understanding adversity in the context of cancer requires a shift in perspective. Rather than seeing challenges as insurmountable, individuals can view them as opportunities for personal growth. Cancer, despite its hardships, can catalyze resilience, deeper connections, and a newfound appreciation for life. By understanding the inherent adversity in a cancer diagnosis, individuals can tap into inner strength and develop coping mechanisms beyond immediate challenges.

Embracing flexibility in thought processes and daily routines becomes crucial to coping with the evolving nature of the disease. It involves adapting to treatment plans, accommodating physical changes, and being open to emotional fluctuations. This flexibility empowers individuals to find joy in small victories, maintain a positive mindset, and build a support network for overall healing.

When people with cancer travel to another country or state for treatment, they face a bunch of challenges. It's not just about different healthcare and language issues – there's also the stress of travel, handling medical bills, and feeling emotionally strained away from their usual support.

But there are ways to deal with these problems. Joining local support groups or online communities can offer advice on navigating foreign healthcare. Language apps and translation services can help with understanding, and learning about new cultures in advance can make adapting easier. Financial aid, like medical travel grants or crowd funding, can ease the money worries. Staying connected with loved ones through video calls provides emotional support. And getting advice from healthcare pros and social workers can offer practical help and coping tips.

Travelling for treatment is tough, but with the right support, it can be a bit easier.

Bringing a caregiver along for cancer treatment abroad is super important. Firstly, they give emotional support, being there for the patient during tough times and making things a bit easier. Practically, a caregiver helps with lots of stuff. Figuring out a new healthcare system, dealing with language differences, and understanding treatment plans can be confusing. A caregiver can sort out appointments, talk to doctors, and make sure the patient gets the care they need. A caregiver is also like a champion for the patient. They can speak up about concerns, ask questions, and make sure the treatment plan suits the patient's preferences and well-being. Plus, if something unexpected happens, having a caregiver around is a big help. Whether it's going to appointments or handling everyday tasks, a caregiver makes a big difference in how comfortable and well-supported the patient feels during cancer treatment abroad

Within the challenges of cancer, hidden opportunities for personal development and growth emerge. Resilience built through adapting to adversity becomes a source of strength. Connections with healthcare professionals, support groups, and loved ones create a network of solidarity beyond the physical aspects of the disease. Embracing change and challenges in the cancer journey can lead to profound transformations, where individuals discover their capabilities and develop a renewed sense of purpose.

The cancer journey is undoubtedly fraught with adversity, but within these challenges lays the potential for profound growth and resilience. Adapting to adversity, understanding its impact, and embracing flexibility become powerful tools for individuals facing cancer. By viewing challenges as opportunities and finding strength in flexibility, individuals can navigate their journey with courage, grace, and a renewed appreciation for the richness of life.

In the journey of cancer, individuals adapt to adversity through small victories during chemotherapy, maintaining a positive mindset. They see cancer as an opportunity for personal growth, forming deeper connections, and appreciating life. Embracing flexibility involves adjusting to treatment, and welcoming physical changes, within challenges; opportunities arise for forming lasting connections with healthcare professionals, leading to personal transformation. In conclusion, embracing flexibility becomes a source of strength, allowing individuals to navigate the cancer journey with courage and a renewed appreciation for life.

Empowered Progress

Engage in meaningful activities, set realistic goals, and celebrate victories to foster fulfilment and success.

"Whenever the victory shines, however small it seems, in each step of success, it fuels our hopeful dreams"

Facing cancer is an immense challenge, both physically and emotionally. In this difficult journey, individuals often find solace and strength in meaningful activities, spending time with loved ones, and exploring new interests. These pursuits bring joy and purpose, making it easier to cope with the rigors of cancer treatment.

Setting realistic goals is pivotal in the cancer journey. Instead of fixating solely on the overarching goal of remission, breaking it into smaller, achievable milestones, such as completing a treatment round or reaching specific health goals, proves essential. These attainable goals boost motivation and contribute to building resilience in the face of adversity.

Celebrating victories, no matter how modest is a fundamental component of empowered progress in the cancer journey.

Small victories for cancer patients can include completing a round of treatment, reaching a milestone in their recovery, experiencing a day with reduced pain or fatigue, or receiving positive news from medical tests. Celebrating these moments helps maintain hope and resilience during the challenging journey.

Positive responses to treatment, improved energy levels, or effectively managing side effects—all these steps forward deserve recognition. Celebrations not only acknowledge individual strength but also create a sense of community, bringing together friends, family, and healthcare providers in support.

In essence, finding empowerment amid the challenges of cancer involves engaging in meaningful activities, setting achievable goals, and celebrating every small triumph. This trifecta establishes a resilient foundation, allowing individuals to confront the hardships of cancer with determination and hope. By fostering a culture of celebration and acknowledging progress, no matter how incremental, we pave the way for a more positive and empowered cancer experience.

When faced with the challenging journey of battling cancer, it is crucial to engage in meaningful activities, set realistic goals and expectations, and celebrate every victory along the way. Cancer, a formidable opponent that affects millions worldwide, not only takes a toll on the physical body but also the mental and emotional well-being of the individual. Therefore, adopting a positive mindset and focusing on activities that bring joy and purpose can greatly contribute to the overall well-being of the cancer patient.

Engaging in meaningful activities is essential to maintain a sense of purpose and fulfilment during the cancer journey. These activities can vary from person to person, depending on their interests and abilities. For some, it may involve pursuing a hobby or passion that brings them happiness and distraction from their illness. For others, it may be engaging in volunteer work or supporting a cause related to cancer research or patient advocacy. By participating in activities that hold significance to them, cancer patients can find a sense of normalcy amidst the challenges they face.

Facing cancer is tough, but diving into what you love can make the journey a bit brighter. It's not just about distraction; it's like a secret weapon, giving you power and helping you feel better. Doing what you're passionate about, whether it's drawing, a hobby, or work stuff, connects you with yourself. In the middle of treatments and uncertainties, doing things you love gives your mind a break. It lets you forget the hard stuff for a while and find comfort in what makes you happiest. Your passions also help you remember who you are. Cancer might try to change how you see yourself, but doing what you love lets you say, "I'm still me." It brings back a sense of normal and gives you a purpose outside of being sick. This not only helps you stay positive but also helps you heal in every way. Passions also bring people together. Whether it's art, sports, or shared interests, doing what you love means you're not alone. Being around people who get it, who love the same things, makes you feel like you belong. This support is super important for keeping your spirits up and not feeling so lonely. And guess what? Doing what you love isn't just good for your mind; it's good for your body too. Studies show that being happy and doing things that make you feel good can boost your immune system. It's like your emotions and your body team up to help you feel better overall. So, when cancer tries to bring you down, remember to find strength in what you love. It helps you stay strong, be yourself, find friends who get it and even helps your body fight back. It's not just a hobby; it's a superpower for getting through tough

Setting realistic goals and expectations is equally important when fighting cancer. While it is crucial to remain hopeful and optimistic, it is also essential to acknowledge the limitations that come with the disease. Setting small and attainable goals can provide a sense of accomplishment and motivation. Whether it is completing a short walk, reading a chapter of a book, or spending quality time with loved ones, every goal achieved brings a sense of victory and boosts morale. By managing expectations and celebrating even the smallest achievements, cancer patients can find strength and motivation to continue their fight.

In the battle against cancer, victories come in various forms - from completing a gruelling round of treatment to reaching a milestone in the recovery process. It is essential to celebrate these victories, regardless of their size, as they signify progress and resilience. Celebrations can be as simple as spending time with loved ones, indulging in a favourite treat, or expressing gratitude for the support received along the journey. By recognizing and acknowledging these victories, cancer patients can find solace and strength in their fight.

In conclusion, engaging in meaningful activities, setting realistic goals and expectations, and celebrating victories are vital components of the cancer journey. By actively participating in activities that bring joy and purpose, cancer patients can maintain a sense of normalcy and fulfilment. Setting realistic goals allows for a sense of accomplishment and motivation, while celebrating victories, big or small, provides a boost in morale and resilience. By adopting these practices, individuals battling cancer can strive towards a more positive and fulfilling life, even in the face of adversity.

Beyond Pain

Coping and Distraction Strategies in the Face of Cancer.

"In the lane of cancer your journey may be full of pain, with each battle fought with tears you will definitely win and gain."

Receiving a cancer diagnosis is undoubtedly a life-altering experience, marked by physical discomfort and emotional distress. However, amidst the challenges of the disease, individuals often discover the power of coping mechanisms and distraction strategies that extend beyond the realm of pain.

Coping with cancer involves navigating not only the physical symptoms but also the psychological and emotional toll it takes. Emotional well-being becomes a crucial aspect of the journey, and individuals often find solace in various coping strategies. Seeking support from friends, family, or support groups provides an outlet for expressing emotions and sharing experiences. Additionally, engaging in mindfulness practices, such as meditation or yoga, proves effective in promoting emotional resilience and a sense of inner calm.

Distraction becomes a valuable ally in alleviating the burden of pain and discomfort associated with cancer. Immersing oneself in activities that bring joy, whether it's pursuing hobbies, enjoying nature, or indulging in creative endeavours, helps shift the focus away from the challenges of the disease. Distraction strategies not only provide relief from physical pain but also contribute to a positive mindset, fostering a sense of normalcy amid the medical complexities.

The support of healthcare providers is instrumental in guiding individuals through effective pain management. Medications, therapies, and alternative treatments are often tailored to address the specific needs and sensitivities of each patient. Open communication with healthcare professionals ensures a collaborative approach, empowering individuals to actively participate in their pain management plan.

Moreover, the emotional support of loved ones plays a pivotal role in enhancing coping mechanisms. The encouragement, understanding, and companionship of friends and family create a robust support network that bolsters resilience. Simple acts of kindness, empathy, and being present for someone facing cancer can significantly impact their ability to cope with the physical and emotional toll.

Explore mindfulness practices for pain perception management. Consider complementary therapies like acupuncture or acupressure. Seek massage therapy for relaxation and muscle tension relief. Apply heat packs or cold compresses per healthcare advice. Collaborate with palliative care teams for holistic symptom management. Work with psychologists for emotional impact through cognitive-behavioural therapy. Maintain a well-balanced diet to potentially alleviate some pain. Incorporate doctor-approved exercises for improved mood and strength. Ensure proper hydration to prevent exacerbated discomfort. Openly communicate changes in pain levels for timely adjustments.

Practice Mindfulness Meditation by Focusing on being present in the moment, and observing thoughts and sensations without judgment. Cultivates feelings of compassion and goodwill toward oneself and others, which can be particularly beneficial for managing the emotional challenges of cancer.

Guided Imagery Involves visualizing positive outcomes or healing images, which may help reduce anxiety and promote relaxation during cancer treatments. Breathe Awareness Meditation Focusing on the breath is a way to anchor attention and promote relaxation, which can help manage stress and improve overall well-being.

Transcendental Meditation which Involves silently repeating a mantra to achieve a state of deep relaxation and inner peace, potentially reducing stress and enhancing resilience in cancer patients. Each type of meditation offers unique benefits that can complement traditional cancer treatments and support the holistic well-being of patients.

Practicing guided meditation can mitigate or divert pain by promoting relaxation, easing muscle tension, and redirecting focus away from the sensation of pain. Guided meditation is a technique wherein a soothing voice leads an individual through a serene and calming exploration, fostering relaxation, and nurturing mindfulness. It often involves visualization, profound breathing, and intentional focus on the current moment. This can enhance awareness and well-being, reduce stress, and promote a sense of inner peace.

Surround yourself with a supportive network for emotional backing. Learn about your cancer type, empowering participation in decisions about pain management

In conclusion, Coping and Distraction Strategies in the Face of Cancer" delves into the multifaceted approach individuals adopt when confronted with a cancer diagnosis. Coping mechanisms, ranging from emotional support to mindfulness practices, address the holistic impact of the disease. Simultaneously, distraction strategies, rooted in engaging activities and creative pursuits, provide relief from the physical burden. Together, these approaches empower individuals to navigate the complexities of cancer with resilience, fostering a sense of hope and normalcy beyond the pain.

Fuelling the Fight and Nourishing to Flourish

Nurturing strategies for sustaining
strength and growth.

"In cancer's quest, let nutrition be your zest, a rhyme of health, on this journey, invest."

Getting good nutrition from food and the diet we consume is a vital aspect of health and wellness, especially for those who are going through a turbulent journey of cancer. Every individual journey through cancer is different and has their unique path. Hence the nutrition goals and diet plans are based on factors like the type of cancer, its stages, and other health conditions. Cancer treatments bring side effects due to some conventional medical treatments which hampers the nutrition of an individual. The affected area after surgery, radiation therapy, side effects from chemotherapy, and other treatments can affect the sense of taste, smell, and appetite, which can make eating and digestion and also in some cases excretion challenging.

To ensure proper and required nutrition as per individual needs while going through treatment, a registered dietician dedicated to the food of cancer becomes essential in supporting the health care team.

Malnutrition became a major cause of concern when it weakens the body's immune system making it difficult to fight infection. Focusing on nourishment individuals and its health care support with family members can enhance their resilience and overall quality of life throughout their cancer journey.

Also being aware of thoughts and feelings related to food and making intentional choices in these practices can help develop a healthier relationship with food. Mindful eating involves savouring each bite, recognizing hunger and fullness clues, and being aware of emotional triggers for eating, incorporating mindfulness into your diet by paying attention and appreciating flavours and textures can foster a healthier relationship with food, aiding in both physical and mental well-being.

The above practices can contribute to better digestion, improved satisfaction from a meal, and a more balanced approach to overall well-being.

The relationship between food and mental well-being is crucial, especially during the journey through cancer.

A proper balanced nutritional diet can provide essential micro and macronutrients that support overall health and may positively influence mood.

Nowadays, foods are loaded with insecticides, pesticides, hence avoid over-processed food and try to implement and accept organic food in your diet

During the cancer journey, it is crucial to avoid external cuisine as it is vital for maintaining a controlled, regulated, and tailored personalized diet.

Crafting meals at home empowers you to oversee ingredients, guaranteeing alignment with your nutritional requirements and dietary limitations. This proactive strategy enhances your overall well-being and contributes to better outcomes throughout the treatment process.

Emphasize a balanced approach to nourishment. Include whole foods like fresh fruits, vegetables, whole grains, and legumes. Embrace super food and spices like turmeric, ginger, and cumin for their potential health benefits. Prioritize a variety of colors and flavours to support overall well-being and consider mindful eating practices for a holistic approach to nutrition.

Also, it's important to monitor nutritional status through blood tests to promptly address and manage nutritional deficiencies.

Polyphenols found in various plant-based foods have been studied for their potential anti-cancer properties. These compounds, including quercetin, kaempferol, catechins, resveratrol, curcumin, ellagic acid, lignans, genistein, anthocyanins, and epigallocatechin gallate, are present in fruits, vegetables, tea, red wine, berries, pomegranates, nuts, flaxseeds, sesame seeds, soybeans, and more. While these polyphenols hold promise, it is crucial to consume them under professional guidance.

But for potential benefit, it's always recommended to consume the same under a professional experienced nutritionist or dietician. Additionally consulting with psychologists can help create a personalised plan to support both physical and mental well-being during the cancer journey.

I believe that "water is life and his life"

It's important to stay hydrated since certain treatment regimens can lead to dehydration. Maintain a healthy weight and posture through regular exercise. Engaging in gentle exercises and activities can have a favourable influence on metabolism and digestion encouraging heightened calorie burn, boosted insulin sensitivity, and improved energy utilization. Integrating these activities into your daily regimen might contribute to a more efficient metabolic process, promoting overall metabolic well-being.

Fasting can be incorporated as part of cancer management to give rest to the digestive system, where an individual follows abstinence from consuming complete or limited certain types of food for a particular period. Fasting can affect individuals differently. It helps eliminate toxins and deposits foreign material from the body. Certain fasting-mimicking diets may have potential benefits such as reducing inflammation and supporting cellular repair, but you should never undertake fasting without proper medical guidance

Smoking and excessive alcohol consumption are known risk factors for various types of cancer, Smoking is strongly linked to lung, throat, and oral cancer among others, and alcohol consumption is said to be associated with an increased risk of cancer in the mouth, throat, oesophagus, liver and breast, Hence, quitting smoking and alcohol completely can reduce the risk of recurrence of cancer.

Be proactive and make more room in your diet for foods that reduce chances and prevent the recurrence of cancer.

Focus on a well-balanced and nutritionally rich approach, including a variety of colourful fruits and vegetables that are high in antioxidants, fibres, and vitamins Opt for whole-grain, lean protein, and healthy fats, Limit sugar, sweetened drinks, Avoid eating raw or uncooked, unpasteurized food, which can harbour several different types of bacteria and many more, Hence avoid them during cancer treatment and recovery, since there is increased risk of full-blown illness on a patient's compromised immune system.

It's essential to be cautious when considering synthetic supplements and nutrition products. Many marketed items make bold claims on social media and television without solid scientific backing; unverified claims may lack scientific evidence. To make informed choices during your treatment, consult with healthcare professionals who can provide evidence-based recommendations tailored to your specific needs.

Financial Assistance and Legal Considerations in the Journey of Cancer

Practical guidance for financial and legal aspects admist a cancer journey.

The journey of cancer is an arduous path laden with physical and emotional challenges, yet the financial burden it imposes on individuals and families adds another layer of complexity to an already difficult situation. The costs associated with cancer diagnosis and treatments have surged to staggering levels, often precipitating a financial crisis for those affected.

Medical expenses, ranging from diagnostic tests to surgeries, chemotherapy, and medications, as well as advanced treatments such as immunotherapy, and targeted therapies are much more costly and are out of reach for many. These expenses can accumulate rapidly, depleting savings and plunging individuals into debt. Even with insurance coverage, out-of-pocket costs, co-pays, and deductibles can be overwhelming. The financial strain extends beyond medical bills, encompassing additional expenses such as transportation to treatment centres, lodging for distant treatments, and childcare during hospital visits.

Furthermore, the impact on employment intensifies the financial crisis. Cancer treatments frequently necessitate time off work for both patients and their caregivers. In some instances, extended absences lead to job loss, resulting in a simultaneous loss of income and health insurance. This creates a domino effect, as the loss of a job can coincide with the loss of employer-sponsored health coverage when it is needed most.

The financial burden persists beyond the immediate treatment phase. Survivors may grapple with ongoing costs related to follow-up care, rehabilitation, and medications. Additionally, the long-term effects of cancer treatments may require lifestyle adjustments, adding further strain on finances.

Addressing the financial burden crisis in the journey of cancer demands a multifaceted approach. Improved access to affordable health insurance, expanded coverage for cancer-related expenses, and financial assistance programs are essential to alleviate economic challenges. Employers play a crucial role by implementing supportive policies for employees undergoing cancer treatment, including flexible work schedules and accommodations.

Community support, through nonprofits organizations and local initiatives, is instrumental in lessening the financial burden. Fundraising efforts, awareness campaigns, and resource-sharing platforms provide much-needed assistance to those facing the economic challenges of cancer. Many people with cancer feel stressed about medical bills. This added financial worry can make their emotional struggles worse, especially for those already dealing with a lot. It's important to offer support, guidance, and counselling before and after cancer surgery to address their emotional distress, anxiety, and depression.

Patients facing financial struggles, especially those with lower incomes, tend to experience more stress about medical costs and cancer-related concerns, to help them, it is crucial to focus on making sure they can access timely oncology care.

Legal considerations encompass estate planning, power of attorney arrangements, and navigating disability benefits. Seeking guidance from financial advisors and legal professionals is advisable to address these intricacies based on individual circumstances.

Various organizations and resources extend financial assistance to individuals grappling with cancer-related financial burdens. Exploring options that can yield financial support or facilitate connections with relevant resources is crucial. Pharmaceutical Assistance Programs, offered by some drug manufacturers, assist with the costs of cancer medications. Government assistance programs may provide additional financial support. Hospital Financial Assistance Programs are available in many medical facilities to aid patients facing financial challenges related to medical bills. Social workers, whether based in hospitals or communities, serve as valuable guides to local resources and assistance programs. Consulting with these resources is recommended for a comprehensive approach to managing the financial and legal complexities associated with cancer.

In conclusion, the financial burden crisis in the journey of cancer is an undeniable reality. As we strive to advance medical treatments and support systems for cancer patients, addressing the economic implications of this devastating disease is equally imperative. Only through collaborative efforts at societal, governmental, and individual levels can we hope to mitigate financial challenges and ensure that individuals facing cancer can focus on healing rather than economic hardships.

Spirituality in the Journey of Cancer

Embracing spiritual resilience on the cancer expedition.

"In the quiet dance of hope and resilience, spirituality becomes the guiding melody in the cancer journey, a source of strength that whispers courage to the soul."

As we approach the culmination of this journey, I offer insights into the spiritual dimensions of cancer, exploring Spirituality in Cancer

Spirituality is a deeply personal journey Individuals' definitions of spirituality are different, the spiritual dimension can be considered as a complimentary medicine where individuals explore their inner selves, seeking meaning in life and connection with something greater than oneself. Spirituality can offer comfort, hope, and a sense of purpose, aiding in coping with emotional and physical challenges in the journey of cancer.

Practices such as religion, meditation or personal reflection play a subjective role in providing strength to many during cancer treatment and recovery.

Religion and spirituality are related concepts but differ in their scope and meaning.

Everyone should have their expression of spirituality. Spiritual and psychological distress can hamper the treatment as well as worsen the symptoms which can lead to depression and anxiety.

The impact of spirituality on cancer outcomes compliments positive influences on mental health, coping mechanisms, and overall quality of life. Emphasizing the need for evidence-based medical treatments alongside spiritual support is must.

Being connected to spirituality or religion can make you feel less stressed and anxious, reducing negative emotions. It also helps combat loneliness, lowering the risk of suicide, and curbing substance abuse. Your heart health may benefit and it aids in adjusting to cancer's impact. During cancer treatment, it enhances the ability to find joy and promotes personal growth. It fosters positive feelings like hope, satisfaction, and inner peace. Importantly, spiritual well-being might even contribute to a longer life. On the flip side, if spiritual distress occurs, seeking support from spiritual leaders can improve health, overall well-being, and coping abilities.

Engaging in spiritual practices during challenging times like cancer can offer emotional and psychological support. Whether through prayer, meditation, or mindfulness, these practices contribute to stress reduction, inner peace, and a positive mindset. Involvement in spiritual communities or seeking guidance from leaders can create a supportive environment. Ultimately, individuals facing cancer should explore practices aligning with their beliefs, finding comfort in moments of difficulty.

Capturing the essence of spirituality by engaging in various practices can have transformative and calming effects, whether through personal or communal rituals, participation in religious traditions, reading sacred texts, connecting with nature, or acts of compassion and service. Spirituality encompasses a diverse range of practices that aim to deepen one's connection with something greater and promote inner peace. The recognition of the divine in nature and the pursuit of purification through rituals contribute to the holistic and transformative nature of spiritual practices.

In cancer care, the medical team acknowledges the personal nature of spirituality. Patients can anticipate their religious beliefs being respected and those finding comfort in spirituality will receive assistance. The healthcare team including doctors and caregivers pays attention to patients' desires and assists with their spiritual needs. This support may involve proposing care goals aligned with their beliefs, endorsing spiritual coping, and connecting them with support groups. Patients can also be directed towards activities like yoga or creative arts programs, recognized for boosting spiritual well-being. Crucially, the healthcare team honour the choices of patients who prefer not to delve into spirituality during their cancer journey.

Eternal Vitality

Exploring ancient wisdom and modern Insights for Better Health.

"Let us honour and open ancient doors while embracing what science has in store. Fusion of both, herbs of old and labs of now, merge harmoniously, to our health vow."

Ayurvedic therapies for cancer aim to balance the body's doshas (Vata, Pitta, Kapha) and strengthen the immune system. Panchakarma, a detoxification process is often used to eliminate toxins. Additionally, specific therapies may include Rasayana (rejuvenation) and external therapies like Abhyanga (oil massage) and Swedana (steam therapy). These practices are personalized based on the individual's, constitution and the type of cancer, but it's crucial to consult with both Ayurvedic practitioners and conventional healthcare providers for a comprehensive treatment plan. Ancient Ayurvedic remedies and herbal treatments have been used for a long time and some people say they've had positive experiences with them. It's okay to consider these traditional approaches to healthcare, especially when guided by the stories of those who found them helpful. Ayurveda an ancient practice from different parts of the world looks at overall well-being and uses natural remedies from herbs.

Talking to someone who has benefited from Ayurvedic medicine can provide useful insights. Their stories can be a good starting point for those looking into alternative treatments. However, it's important to be careful and think critically about this information.

Before trying any Ayurvedic treatments, it's crucial to consult with an experienced Ayurvedic practitioner. These professionals can evaluate your health, suggest personalized treatments, and make sure they won't interfere with any other medical treatments you're undergoing. Ayurvedic practitioners consider not only your symptoms but also your overall lifestyle and well-being.

Ayurveda focuses on balanced and personalized care by using natural elements. The herbs recommended in Ayurveda have a long history of use, but their effectiveness can vary from person to person. While some Ayurvedic practices have some scientific support, it's not as much as conventional medicine. So, a good approach is to combine traditional knowledge with what modern medicine understands.

It's essential to understand that while Ayurvedic remedies may work for some conditions, they may not be a cure for everything. In some cases Ayurvedic treatments can complement Western medicine, offering a more holistic approach to healing.

In conclusion, trying old-aged Ayurvedic medicines and herbs based on positive experiences is okay but has to be done cautiously and under the guidance of a qualified Ayurvedic practitioner. The key is to find a balance between traditional wisdom and modern medical knowledge for a personalized approach to healthcare.

When dealing with health concerns, it's essential to talk to a medical professional before trying any supplements or advertised products, especially for cancer. Healthcare professionals can check for potential issues with ongoing treatments and provide advice based on an individual's medical history to ensure well-being and prevent unintended consequences. Unfortunately, some companies aggressively market anti-cancer therapies without strong scientific support. This trend takes advantage of people facing a cancer diagnosis, potentially risking their health. Many of these products lack rigorous scientific research making their safety and effectiveness questionable.

These unverified cancer therapies add confusion for patients seeking reliable treatments. The emotional stress of a cancer diagnosis might lead individuals to explore alternative options, falling prey to unproven remedies. This could result in delayed or neglected conventional medical treatments putting recovery at risk.

The ethical concerns go further with the financial burden imposed by these promotions. Some therapies come with high costs exploiting the desperation of those seeking a cure. People might invest significant resources in treatments that not only fail to deliver promised results but also worsen their health conditions.

To address this issue, regulatory bodies need to enforce stricter measures against companies making unsupported claims. Healthcare professionals play a crucial role in educating patients about evidence-based treatments and the risks of unverified therapies.

In summary, the promotion of anti-cancer therapies without strong scientific support is concerning. Advocating for evidence-based medicine, reinforcing regulatory measures, and empowering individuals with reliable information are crucial. The focus should always be on the well-being of those facing a cancer diagnosis, ensuring they receive safe and effective treatments supported by sound scientific evidence.

Some companies use emotional appeals to promote cancer-related products, taking advantage of people dealing with a cancer diagnosis. This marketing strategy while effective in capturing attention raises ethical concerns and can have negative consequences for those seeking genuine solutions.

These companies create compelling stories that play on the emotions of individuals and families facing cancer. Emotional messages in still a sense of urgency, making people believe the advertised product is the key to overcoming the illness. This emotional manipulation can cloud judgment, leading individuals to make decisions based on feelings rather than evidence-based reasoning.

Accompanying the emotional appeal are anecdotes and testimonials highlighting apparent success stories. While these narratives may be touching, they often lack scientific validation and can mislead individuals into trusting products that may not deliver promised benefits. Exploiting emotions in marketing cancer-related products adds a significant financial and emotional burden on patients and their support networks.

Healthcare professionals play a crucial role in educating patients about critical evaluation and seeking evidence-based treatments. Empowering individuals with information and promoting media literacy helps navigate emotional marketing tactics, enabling informed decisions about their health.

In essence, the appeal of cancer-related products through emotional marketing underscores the need for heightened consumer awareness, ethical marketing standards, and increased regulatory vigilance. Encouraging evidence-based decision-making enables individuals to better protect themselves from the potential pitfalls of emotionally driven marketing in the context of cancer.

One new type of holistic approach to cancer could be "Ecotherapy Integration." This approach involves incorporating nature-based interventions and environmental connections into cancer care to promote healing and well-being. It recognizes the profound impact that nature can have on physical, emotional, and psychological health and seeks to harness these benefits in the cancer journey.

Ecotherapy Integration offers a holistic approach to cancer care that considers not only the physical and medical aspects of the disease but also the broader connections between individuals, nature, and the environment. By integrating nature-based interventions into cancer treatment and support services, this approach aims to enhance healing, foster resilience, and improve the overall quality of life for those affected by cancer.

Ecotherapy Integration in cancer care may include utilizing Nature-Based Therapies and activities such as forest bathing, gardening, nature walks, and outdoor meditation to promote relaxation, reduce stress, and enhance overall well-being for cancer patients and survivors.

Green Spaces in Healthcare Settings which Design hospitals and treatment centers with access to natural light, greenery, and outdoor spaces to create healing environments that support recovery and provide respite from the clinical setting.

Therapeutic Gardens creates gardens specifically designed to meet the needs of cancer patients, with features such as sensory gardens, healing landscapes, and spaces for reflection and contemplation.

Animal-assisted therapy Incorporates interactions with animals, such as therapy dogs or equine therapy, to provide comfort, companionship, and emotional support for individuals undergoing cancer treatment.

Environmental Awareness and Advocacy educating patients, caregivers, and healthcare providers about the connections between environmental health and cancer risk, as well as promoting advocacy efforts to address environmental factors that contribute to cancer incidence and disparities.

Do and Don'ts for Resilience and Well-being

The journey continues with insightful advice on navigating the intricate landscape of Do's and Don'ts in Cancer, laying the foundation for informed decision-making.

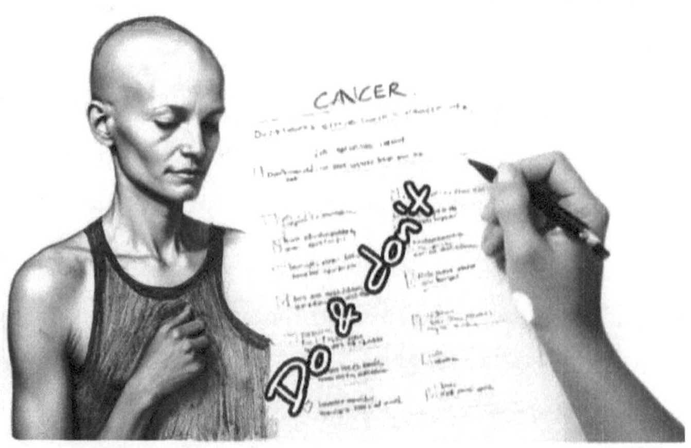

Do's for Patients Going Through a Cancer Journey:

1. Do Seek Professional Guidance. Consult with oncologists and healthcare professionals for personalized advice and treatment plans.

2. Do Build a Support Network. Surround yourself with family and friends who can provide emotional and practical support.

3. Do educate yourself. Learn about your specific type of cancer, treatment options and potential side effects to make informed decisions.

4. Do communicate openly. Share your feelings and concerns with your healthcare team, family and friends to ensure a supportive environment.

5. Do prioritize self-care. Take time for activities that bring you joy and relaxation to maintain overall well-being.

6. Do Consider Second Opinions. If needed, seek second opinions to ensure you explore all available treatment options.

7. Do keep Records. Maintain a record of medical information, treatment plans, and any questions you may have for healthcare providers.

8. Do Stay Active. Engage in gentle exercises or activities suitable for your condition to enhance physical and mental well-being.

9. Do Attend Support Groups. Joining cancer support groups can provide valuable insights, empathy, and shared experiences.

10. Do Address Financial concerns .seek assistance from financial counsellors or support organizations to manage potential financial challenges.

11. Do Foster Positivity. Surround yourself with positive influences and engage in activities that uplift your spirits.

12. Do Explore Complementary Therapies. Consider complementary therapies like yoga, meditation, or acupuncture to complement traditional treatments

13. Do Maintain a Healthy Diet. Focus on a balanced and nutritious diet to support your body's strength and resilience.

14. Do Involve Caregivers. Keep caregivers informed and involved, allowing them to provide valuable assistance and emotional support.

15. Do Celebrate Milestones. Acknowledge and celebrate small victories and milestones in your treatment journey.

16. Do Keep a Journal. Document your thoughts and experiences in a journal to help process emotions and track your progress.

17. Do Set Realistic Goals. Establish achievable goals to maintain a sense of purpose and accomplishment

18. Do Express Creativity. Engage in creative outlets, such as art or writing, as a therapeutic means of self-expression.

19. Do Stay Informed About Support Services. Be aware of available support services, including counselling, transportation assistance and community resources.

20. Do Lean on Faith or Spirituality. Draw strength from your faith or spirituality to find comfort and resilience.

Don'ts for Patients Going Through a Cancer Journey:

1. Don't Neglect Emotional Well-being. Acknowledge and address emotional challenges by seeking counselling or support services.

2. Don't isolate yourself. Stay connected with loved ones and communicates your needs to maintain a supportive network.

3. Don't Skip Appointments. Attend all medical appointments and follow-ups to stay informed about your treatment progress.

4. Don't Rely Solely on Internet information. While information is valuable, consult your healthcare team for accurate and personalized guidance.

5. Don't Ignore Symptoms. Report any new symptoms or concerns promptly to your healthcare providers for timely intervention.

6. Don't Hesitate to Ask Questions. Always ask your healthcare team questions to clarify doubts and make informed decisions.

7. Don't Rush Decision .take the time you need to make treatment decisions and seek additional opinions if necessary.

8. Don't Over commit. Manage your energy levels and avoid taking on too many commitments during treatment.

9. Don't Disregard Nutrition .intake a balanced diet to support your body during treatment and recovery.

10. Don't Forget Legal and Financial Planning. Consider legal and financial aspects, such as advanced directives and wills for future peace of mind.

11. Don't Ignore Fatigue. Pay attention to your body's signals and rest when needed to manage fatigue effectively.

12. Don't Disregard Mental Health. Prioritize mental health and seek professional help if necessary to cope with stress and anxiety.

13. Don't Compare Journeys. Avoid comparing your cancer journey to others; each experience is unique.

14. Don't engage in Self-Blame. Understand that a cancer diagnosis is not your fault, and focus on moving forward positively

15. Don't Bottle Up Emotions. Express your feelings regularly to prevent emotional build-up and promote mental well-being.

16. Don't Neglect Physical Activity. Incorporate gentle exercises into your routine to maintain physical strength and flexibility.

17. Don't Fear Seeking Help. Reach out for assistance when needed, whether it's for household chores or emotional support

18. Don't overanalyze. Avoid excessive internet research; rely on your healthcare team for accurate and personalized information.

19. Don't Forget Mind-Body Connection. Recognize the interconnectedness of mental and physical well-being and address both aspects.

20. Don't Lose Hope. Maintain a positive outlook and seek inspiration from stories of resilience to cultivate hope throughout your journey.

Beyond the Battle

Narratives of Triumph and Life after Cancer

"Gone are the days of shadows and sorrow, in their wake, emerges a bright tomorrow. With cancer conquered, you have unlocked the key, now let your spirit soar, unbound and free!"

Getting diagnosed with cancer is tough and can be a long, hard journey involving physical, emotional, and mental challenges. But the story doesn't end with the struggle; it goes on to tales of success and the happy life that comes after beating cancer. Life after cancer is marked by a unique blend of resilience, gratitude, and newfound perspectives.

After cancer people experience a mix of strength, thankfulness, and a new way of looking at things, those who beat cancer often become storytellers, sharing their journeys as stories of success. These stories bring hope and courage to others going through a similar tough time proving that life can be good even after a difficult battle.

Beating cancer isn't just about medical victories; it includes the emotional and mental strength gained during the journey. Survivors often talk about personal growth, new strengths, and a greater appreciation for life that comes from facing mortality. These changes shape a story that goes beyond the struggle, painting a picture of a more vibrant and meaningful life.

Getting back to a normal life becomes a big part of life after cancer. Reclaiming a sense of normalcy becomes a significant aspect of life after cancer. People find joy in everyday moments, appreciating the simplicity of regular activities that they used to take for granted. Mundane things become special and survivors often embrace a fresh enthusiasm for life, guided by a deeper understanding of its fragility and preciousness.

The support system around cancer survivors plays a crucial role in shaping their stories after treatment. Family, friends, and healthcare providers become important characters in tales of success. Their steady support during the battle and afterward contributes to creating a story that celebrates not just individual strength but also the collective resilience of the community.

Life after Beating Cancer highlights how life continues beyond the challenges of cancer. It explores the experiences of survivors who after facing tough times, find a new love for life, share their success stories, and journey a path full of hope, strength, and the embrace of simple yet wonderful moments. These stories remind us that life after cancer is not just a continuation but a testament to the strength of the human spirit and the beauty of the journey beyond the struggle.

Beating cancer is undoubtedly a monumental achievement, signifying resilience, courage, and triumph over adversity. However, the journey towards holistic well-being doesn't conclude with the victory over cancer; rather, it emphasizes the importance of maintaining a comprehensive and holistic approach to health.

During the battle with cancer, individuals often adopt a holistic mindset that encompasses physical, emotional, and mental well-being. This holistic approach involves not only medical treatments but also lifestyle adjustments, emotional support, and mental resilience. It is crucial to recognize that the principles guiding this holistic mindset should persist post-cancer as well.

Firstly, physical well-being remains a cornerstone of a holistic approach. Practices such as regular exercise, a balanced diet, and adequate sleep, which were likely integral during cancer treatment, should persist. Engaging in activities that promote overall physical health not only supports the body's recovery but also contributes to long-term wellness.

Emotional well-being is another vital aspect that should continue to receive attention. The emotional toll of a cancer diagnosis and treatment is substantial and strategies such as counselling support groups and mindfulness that aid in emotional resilience should be sustained. Prioritizing mental health fosters a positive mindset, aiding in the transition to a fulfilling life after cancer.

Moreover, the support network that played a pivotal role during the cancer journey remains invaluable post-treatment. Family, friends, and healthcare providers continue to contribute significantly to overall well-being. Also maintaining open communication and seeking support when needed form essential elements of a holistic approach, fostering a sense of connection and understanding.

Cultivating a healthy lifestyle extends beyond the medical realm, encompassing mental and emotional aspects. Engaging in activities that bring joy, pursuing hobbies, and nurturing relationships contribute to a more fulfilling post-cancer life. The pursuit of passions and the enjoyment of life's simple pleasures remain integral components of holistic well-being.

Ensuring a cancer-free future involves sustaining a wholesome lifestyle. Periodic check-ups, embracing a well-rounded diet, staying physically active, managing stress, and steering clear of tobacco and excessive alcohol also contribute to minimizing the likelihood of a recurrence.

As a cancer survivor learned that cancer is intricate, influenced by factors like genetic mutations, environment (tobacco smoke, UV radiation), lifestyle choices (diet, physical activity), and exposure to carcinogens (pesticides, industrial chemicals, alcohol, radiation). Interactions among these factors heighten the risk of cancer. Individuals facing this journey should urge everyone to minimize exposure through healthy lifestyle choices, regular screenings, and awareness, helping mitigate the risks of occurrence and recurrence. Let's empower each other to make informed decisions for a healthier future.

In essence, the holistic approach adopted during the battle with cancer should not be discarded but rather integrated into the fabric of post-cancer life. Embracing physical, emotional, and mental well-being as interconnected elements ensures a more robust foundation for a fulfilling and healthy life beyond cancer. By persisting in these holistic practices, individuals can continue to thrive, embracing the newfound appreciation for life that the cancer journey has imparted while maintaining a comprehensive approach to overall wellness.

Witnessing a loved one battle cancer can be incredibly difficult. Creating awareness, promoting prevention measures and steps, and offering support programs are essential steps in combating cancer as a society. By educating and creating awareness among people about the importance of early detection, healthy lifestyles, and available resources for those affected by cancer, we can help reduce its prevalence and alleviate the suffering of individuals and families. Support programs provide emotional, practical, and financial assistance to those undergoing treatment, as well as their caregivers. Together, through collective efforts and solidarity, we can make a significant impact in the fight against cancer.

www.ingramcontent.com/pod-product-compliance
Lightning Source LLC
Chambersburg PA
CBHW031303130726

47988CB00007B/2714